CONTENTS

Introduction	1
The PASS method	2
The Thesis	4
Examples - Thesis statements for A Christmas Carol	12
Examples - PASS Analytical paragraph	18
Extend - Universal Concepts in A Christmas Carol	33
Extend - Historical context	41
Extend - Dickens' methods	46
Extend - Structural Decisions in A Christmas Carol	52
Practise - Gap-Fill Exercises	61
Practise - Analyse language Step-by-step	66
Revision - Thesis building questions	70
Revision - Example Essays	72

INTRODUCTION

This book is designed to help year 10 and 11 students currently studying for English Literature GCSE with AQA. It is designed to support specifically with A Christmas Carol.

What Can This Book Do For Me?

Inside this book you will find straightforward explanations from an experienced English teacher that will add to what you already know about how to pass the GCSE English Literature exam. You will build on your existing understanding and pick up ways to boost your marks for each question. If you are currently sitting on a grade 3 or 4, this book can help boost your answers and lift your grade.

What Can't This Book Do For Me?

This book cannot do the exam for you, and it cannot match the value of the time you spend in the classroom. It is not intended teach you the entire text – it is a supplement to what you already know. Trust your teachers, trust yourself, and use this book as an extra layer of support.

THE PASS METHOD

What is the PASS method?

The PASS method is a simple structure for you to follow when writing literature essays in the exam. The PASS method helps you to:

- Explain your answer to the question clearly

and
- Explore the language in the text clearly

This will secure a 'clear' response and therefore a GCSE pass.

Moving up: The PASS method can also help you to reach the highest level of a thoughtful, conceptual and perceptive response, by helping you to:

- Make conceptual links to fundamental human emotions and experiences

How does it work?

The PASS method works on the basis of giving you 7 levels to work through in order to make your answers as clear as possible.

Can I use the PASS method for all my English literature exams?

The PASS method can be used towards 100% of the marks in your English Literature GCSE exams.

When and how to use the PASS method in your language GCSE papers:

Paper 1

Shakespeare question – Thesis and PASS analytical paragraph
19TH Century text question – Thesis and PASS analytical paragraph

Paper 2

Modern text question – Thesis and PASS analytical paragraph
Anthology poetry question – Thesis and 2 X PASS analytical paragraphs
Unseen poetry question – Thesis and PASS analytical paragraph
Unseen poetry comparison question – 1 or 2 PASS analytical paragraphs

What does the PASS method look like?

In brief, the PASS method looks like this:

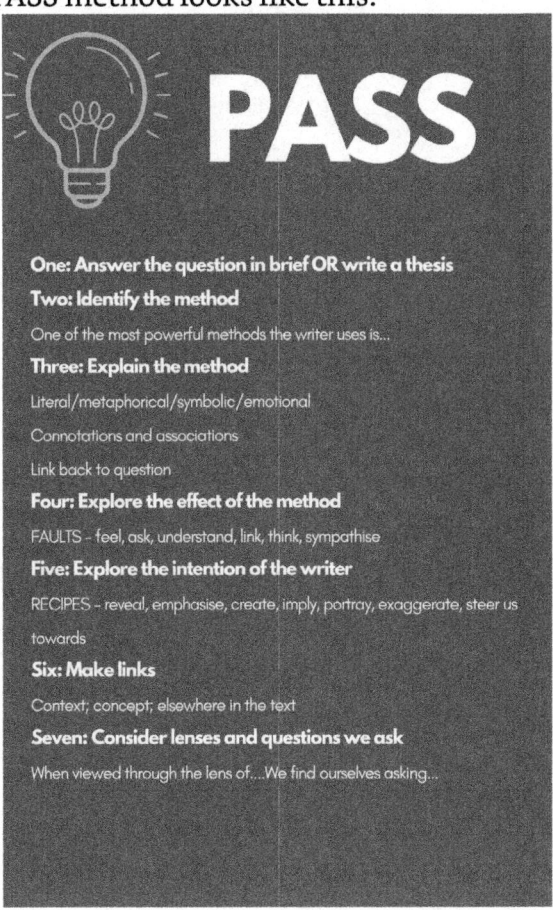

One: Answer the question in brief OR write a thesis

Two: Identify the method

One of the most powerful methods the writer uses is...

Three: Explain the method

Literal/metaphorical/symbolic/emotional

Connotations and associations

Link back to question

Four: Explore the effect of the method

FAULTS - feel, ask, understand, link, think, sympathise

Five: Explore the intention of the writer

RECIPES - reveal, emphasise, create, imply, portray, exaggerate, steer us towards

Six: Make links

Context; concept; elsewhere in the text

Seven: Consider lenses and questions we ask

When viewed through the lens of....We find ourselves asking...

THE THESIS

A thesis response is a detailed and conceptual introduction to your answer. You should begin all of your literature essays with a thesis.

Giving a thesis response means that you can explore a more conceptual approach before considering the methods used by the writer in your analytical paragraph.

The picture above can be used as a guide to help remember the stages of the thesis. You can do a doodle version on your exam paper to remind you of the steps, which are:

Journey (the road)

The end of the text (horizon)

Mood (sun)

Universal concepts and conflict (bushy trees and spikey trees)

Lenses and questions (magnifying glass/letter Q)

By including each of these elements in your thesis response, you can achieve marks for comments on the big ideas, on mood, and on structure, without even looking for a specific 'method' yet. You are showing you understand the text as a whole, which is a higher order skill and shows you are viewing it as a construct.

The Journey

Think of every story like a journey. Where do we begin, where do we go, and where do we end up? Every story ever written, every film ever made, every TV series, every song, every painting...they all have stories to tell through a specific journey.

Your job is to identify the journey we are on in the text given. Sometimes it will be a journey specific to you; a journey of discovery of a new idea about life or a new angle to life that you hadn't previously considered. Sometimes it will be a journey that the character goes on, that we experience alongside.

The End

By considering the end of the text, you will be automatically discussing structure. By analysing where we are 'left' at the end of a piece of writing, a film, or a song, you will be halfway towards analysing the creator's intention. What do we understand by the end that we didn't know before, about the characters, or situation, or humanity, or the world?

The Mood

Every piece of writing has a mood. Think of the mood as the vibe or feeling created by external forces. These external forces are ALL down to the writer. The weather, the setting, the events, the characters...all of these elements affect the mood of a piece, and all of them have been created by someone's mind.

Therefore, by writing about the mood you are, once again, analysing the writer's intentions and methods without explicitly zooming in on any one 'technique' yet. This, again, shows your understanding of the piece as a whole.

When writing about mood, especially in poetry, look for how the mood fluctuates, or changes. Again, this will show that you are able to analyse the effect of a writer's choices. When it comes to deeper analysis, you can explore HOW the writer created that mood - but your first job is to identify it in the thesis.

Universal Concepts

Every story ever created, in whatever format, has universal concepts within in. The very best stories can be understood no matter where you are in the world. No matter your background, everyone can relate to love, hatred, jealousy, greed, hope, discovery, youth, leadership etc.

Your job in studying English, from GCSE all the way through university level, is to look at what concepts the writer is asking us to consider. Most of the time, these concepts will have dictated the language used, the setting, the characters, the plot...so working out what the concepts are is key to understanding the writer's choices.

The Conflict

Most stories have some sort of conflict within them. It might be between a character, between two states of being, between light and shade, nature and man, young and old. Your job is to look for the conflict and explore that in the context of the big ideas or concepts of the story.

You can then see if the conflict is resolved at the end - thereby talking about structure and intention and achieving higher marks through viewing the text as a construct.

Lenses And Questions

This level can work very well for literature texts, but can also be relevent for the language exams. Our view of a text is influenced by the metaphorical lens through which we view it; our viewpoint and understanding of Romeo and Juliet, for example, is very different if we look at it through the eyes of a teenager as opposed to an adult. It is different again if we look at it through the eyes of a feminist, or a father.

By thinking about different lenses through which a text can be viewed, you will be exploring higher order ideas and analysing the impact and effect of a writer's choices on a whole new level.

A student called Imogen gave me the idea of finishing a thesis with a question. She used to do this every time and it worked so well, the class and I made it part of standard practice. Finishing with a question shows the examiner that you have engaged with the text to the point where you are able to view it beyond the page.

What do we wonder about the character, the author, the audience? What do we find ourselves asking, rhetorically or otherwise, at the end of the text?

Sentence Starters For Your Thesis

In this extract/poem/novel/play we go on a journey of understanding that
By the end we can see that the writer may have wanted to
The mood of the extract/poem/novel/play fluctuates between
And in doing so introduces the idea of the universal concept(s) of...because...
There is conflict between.....which is/is not resolved by the end
When viewed through the lens of...
Ultimately, we find ourselves asking...

After completing your thesis, you would then complete an analytical PASS paragraph, which looks at the most powerful method that led you to your conclusion in your thesis.

Universal Concepts, Relationships And Fears.

Here are some examples of universal concepts, relationships, and fears that you can usually find in any piece of writing. These can be used when writing a thesis response. They are also good revision tools for the literature GCSE, too. Try and link different characters to the concepts, either because they are representative of that concept, or antithetical to it.

There are hundreds of these that you can find but the examples below are a good place to start.

Universal Concepts/Dualities

Freedom and restriction
Innocence and corruption
Dreams and reality
Love and hate

Safety and danger
Truth and lies

Universal Relationships

Young and old
Rich and poor
Leader and follower
Lost and found
Effort and reward
Endings and beginnings
Nature and man

Universal Fears

Loss
Death
Money
Isolation
Abandonment
isolation
Disenfranchisement

Universal ideas like these allow us to relate to a text, to identify with the writer or character, and to empathise and sympathise with a situation or problem. There are many more ideas you can consider as well as those above, but these are a good place to start.

Practise using them by looking for elements of them in things you read, or films or tv programmes that you watch. You can even find them in songs you listen to.

Exploring these in your thesis can lead you towards a conceptual response, which is what distinguishes a higher grade answer.

Example Thesis Using Little Red Riding Hood

In Little Red Riding Hood, we go on a journey of understanding

EXAMPLES - THESIS STATEMENTS FOR A CHRISTMAS CAROL

These are examples of thesis statements for A Christmas Carol. They are not exhaustive, and are intended to be used as springboards for your own ideas. The activities in the back of this book will prompt your own thoughts too.

While reading them, revise your knowledge of the play by thinking about moments from the play, and quotes, that would provide evidence to support each thesis.

In the exam, your job is to write a thesis response to the question, and then provide evidence for your theory using the text in the extract and in the whole play.

Whichever theme or character comes up in the question, you should be in a position to:

- Know your thoughts on the theme or character
- Be able to present your thoughts in a thesis statement
- Instantly know a couple of moments from the play that works with your thesis (either as a support or antithesis)
- Pick out a quote from the extract that works with your thesis (either as a support or antithesis.)

The Power of Redemption

In *A Christmas Carol*, we go on a journey of understanding how redemption is possible even for those who seem beyond saving. At first, Scrooge is cold-hearted and dismissive of others, believing that the poor are responsible for their own suffering. However, by the end, Dickens may have wanted us to consider that true change requires both self-reflection and action, rather than empty words or regret. The conflict between Scrooge's selfishness and his potential for change is present throughout the novella, but his exposure to past, present, and future suffering forces him to accept responsibility. The universal concepts of guilt, forgiveness, and transformation drive this theme. There is conflict between Scrooge's resistance to change and the possibility of redemption, which is ultimately resolved as he embraces generosity and kindness.

Social Responsibility
In *A Christmas Carol*, we go on a journey of understanding how those with wealth and power have a moral duty to care for others. At first, Scrooge dismisses charity, seeing poverty as a failure of the poor rather than a social issue. However, by the end, Dickens may have wanted us to consider that society can only function if individuals take responsibility for one another, rather than acting out of selfishness or greed. The conflict between self-interest and communal responsibility is evident throughout the novella—Scrooge initially sees profit as the only measure of success, but he later recognises that human connection is more valuable. The universal concepts of wealth, duty, and inequality drive this theme. There is conflict between the capitalist mindset that prioritises profit and the idea that true success is measured by kindness, which is ultimately resolved as Scrooge chooses generosity over greed.

Isolation vs. Community
In *A Christmas Carol*, we go on a journey of understanding how isolation, whether emotional or physical, can destroy happiness and well-being. At first, Scrooge isolates himself from others,

seeing companionship as unnecessary. However, by the end, Dickens may have wanted us to consider that true happiness comes not from wealth but from human connection, and that isolation leads only to regret and loneliness. The conflict between Scrooge's solitude and the warmth of community runs throughout the novella—he rejects family and social interaction, yet the Cratchits and Fezziwigs thrive on love and togetherness. The universal concepts of companionship, regret, and belonging drive this theme. There is conflict between Scrooge's belief that he is better off alone and the reality that he longs for connection, which is ultimately resolved when he embraces Christmas as a time for family and generosity.

Time and Regret
In *A Christmas Carol*, we go on a journey of understanding how time is both a gift and a curse, offering opportunities for change but also the weight of regret. At first, Scrooge believes that time has little significance beyond financial success. However, by the end, Dickens may have wanted us to consider that time should be valued not for productivity, but for how it is spent with others and the impact we leave behind. The conflict between using time for self-interest and using it for meaningful change is central to the novella—Scrooge sees the errors of his past and the bleakness of his future. The universal concepts of opportunity, reflection, and consequence drive this theme. There is conflict between Scrooge's belief that money defines success and the realisation that time spent with loved ones is more important, which is ultimately resolved when he chooses to change his ways before it is too late.

Greed vs. Generosity
In *A Christmas Carol*, we go on a journey of understanding how the pursuit of wealth without compassion leads to misery rather than fulfilment. At first, Scrooge equates financial success with happiness, disregarding those who lack money. However, by the end, Dickens may have wanted us to consider that true wealth is found not in possessions, but in the ability to bring joy to others.

The conflict between greed and generosity is a driving force in the novella—Scrooge hoards wealth but is miserable, while those with little, like the Cratchits, find happiness in love and gratitude. The universal concepts of materialism, fulfilment, and kindness drive this theme. There is conflict between the idea that money provides security and the reality that generosity provides fulfilment, which is ultimately resolved when Scrooge learns that giving to others brings true happiness.

Dickens' most powerful method to convey this is character transformation, as Scrooge's complete shift from miser to benefactor is at the heart of the novella. His willingness to donate money and celebrate Christmas with others symbolises the triumph of generosity over greed.

The Impact of Fear

In *A Christmas Carol*, we go on a journey of understanding how fear can be a catalyst for change but can also paralyse individuals into inaction. At first, Scrooge uses fear to control others—he is feared by his employees and dismissed as cold and unapproachable. However, by the end, Dickens may have wanted us to consider that fear, when confronted, can lead to self-improvement rather than isolation and regret. The conflict between Scrooge's fear of emotional vulnerability and his fear of dying unloved and forgotten is central to the novella—his greatest realisation is that wealth cannot protect him from loneliness. The universal concepts of mortality, self-awareness, and transformation drive this theme. There is conflict between Scrooge's belief that money shields him from harm and the truth that only kindness and connection will give his life meaning, which is ultimately resolved when he embraces generosity as his legacy.

The Corrupting Influence of Wealth

In *A Christmas Carol*, we go on a journey of understanding how the pursuit of wealth, when prioritised over humanity, leads to isolation and moral decay. At first, Scrooge views money as the sole measure of success, dismissing emotions as weaknesses. However, by the end, Dickens may have wanted us to consider that wealth without compassion is meaningless, and that true success is defined by how we treat others. The conflict between financial security and emotional fulfilment is woven throughout the novella—Scrooge hoards wealth but finds no joy in it, while the Cratchits, despite their poverty, find richness in love and gratitude. The universal concepts of greed, generosity, and moral responsibility drive this theme. There is conflict between Scrooge's belief that financial control brings power and the realisation that kindness is far more valuable, which is ultimately resolved when he chooses to give rather than hoard.

Family And Belonging

In *A Christmas Carol*, we go on a journey of understanding how family and human connection provide meaning in life, while isolation leads to regret. At first, Scrooge rejects the idea of family, refusing Fred's invitations and showing no concern for others. However, by the end, Dickens may have wanted us to consider that true happiness comes not from wealth, but from a sense of belonging and love. The conflict between Scrooge's detachment and Fred's unwavering warmth highlights the contrast between isolation and inclusion—Fred offers Scrooge love and companionship, yet Scrooge pushes him away. The universal concepts of love, acceptance, and forgiveness drive this theme. There is conflict between Scrooge's belief that family is an unnecessary burden and the realisation that it is the foundation of true happiness, which is ultimately resolved when he embraces Fred and the Cratchits as his own.

The Past's Influence on the Present

In *A Christmas Carol*, we go on a journey of understanding how the past shapes identity, influencing both choices and regrets. At first, Scrooge resents his past, refusing to acknowledge the pain or joy it contains. However, by the end, Dickens may have wanted us to consider that reflecting on the past is essential for growth, and that avoiding it only leads to stagnation. The conflict between Scrooge's unwillingness to revisit his memories and the necessity of confronting them to move forward is central to the novella—he is forced to witness his lost love, his neglected friendships, and his descent into greed. The universal concepts of memory, regret, and redemption drive this theme. There is conflict between Scrooge's belief that the past is irrelevant and the truth that it holds the key to his transformation, which is ultimately resolved when he embraces its lessons rather than burying them.

The Meaning of Christmas
In *A Christmas Carol*, we go on a journey of understanding how Christmas represents not just a festive celebration, but a time for generosity, reflection, and human kindness. At first, Scrooge dismisses Christmas as a commercial inconvenience, mocking those who celebrate it. However, by the end, Dickens may have wanted us to consider that Christmas is not about material wealth, but about togetherness, charity, and renewal. The conflict between Scrooge's cynicism and the genuine joy of those who embrace the holiday spirit highlights the contrast between greed and goodwill—Fred and the Cratchits celebrate Christmas despite hardship, showing that its true value lies in love and generosity. The universal concepts of joy, renewal, and giving drive this theme. There is conflict between Scrooge's belief that Christmas is a waste of time and the realisation that it is an opportunity for transformation, which is ultimately resolved when he makes the holiday his defining moment of generosity.

EXAMPLES - PASS ANALYTICAL PARAGRAPH

Once you have written your thesis, your next job is to write your analytical paragraphs.

You only need to do one of these to back up your thesis, but you can write more than one if you wish. The reason you only need one is because you are simply choosing the most impactful method to back up the thesis you've already written; your analysis should continue the thought you started in your thesis. This doesn't mean you only use one quote - you can use as many as you wish - it means that you choose one method and explain it in detail and make sure it follows your overall thesis ideas at the beginning.

The Pass Method = Thesis Plus Analytical Paragraph

Your thesis is level one of the method. Here is a detailed breakdown of the remaining six levels of the PASS method, with examples.

Level Two: Name the Method and Quote It
In Level One, you answered the question using the thesis.

As you know, to gain high marks in exams, you must support your argument with evidence from the text.

In the PASS method, the sentence we use to demonstrate our evidence is:

One of the most powerful methods Dickens uses to present the idea of (topic) is (method with quote).

The phrase "one of the most powerful methods" is key, as it shows you have consciously selected a particular technique, evaluated its impact, and determined it to be the most significant for analysis.

Methods can include literary devices such as metaphor, personification, symbolism, contrast, juxtaposition, or even single words, phrases, and semantically linked language.

Tip:

Looking for semantically linked words and explaining their effect will enhance your analysis. Semantically linked words are those with shared connotations or meanings. Some examples from *A Christmas Carol*:

- **Greed and selfishness:** "tight-fisted... grasping... squeezing... covetous"
- **Redemption and transformation:** "light... warmth... generosity... laughter"
- **Isolation and loneliness:** "solitary... neglected... forgotten... abandoned"

Examples of Method Sentences:

- One of the most powerful methods Dickens uses to present Scrooge's miserliness is the use of semantically linked words: "tight-fisted... squeezing... grasping."
- One of the most powerful methods Dickens uses to present the theme of redemption is the symbolism of

light in "I am as light as a feather."
- **One of the most powerful methods Dickens uses to show the contrast between past and present is the personification of time in "the relentless Ghost of Christmas Yet to Come."**

Our paragraph:

In this extract, Dickens presents Scrooge's miserliness as deeply ingrained and all-consuming. One of the most powerful methods Dickens uses to present Scrooge's greed is the use of semantically linked words: "tight-fisted... squeezing... grasping."

Level Three: Explain the Meaning of the Method

Now you have:
- Answered the question briefly in Level One
- Identified a key method in Level Two

In Level Three, you need to explain the meaning of the method. Strong responses layer analysis by considering:

- **Literal, metaphorical, and symbolic meanings**
- **Connotations and associations of specific words**
- **Links to the question to clarify how the quote develops the theme**

Tip:

Use the word "because" frequently. Do not assume the examiner will infer your point—explain it explicitly.

Example of Method Explanation:

In this extract, Dickens presents Scrooge's miserliness as deeply ingrained and all-consuming. One of the most powerful methods Dickens uses to present Scrooge's greed is the use of semantically linked words: "tight-fisted... squeezing... grasping. Literally, these words suggest Scrooge's obsession with money—he clings to wealth as if physically unable to part with it. The verb "squeezing" connotes excessive control, as if Scrooge is wringing every last penny from those around him. Metaphorically, this highlights Scrooge's emotional poverty, as he hoards money but lacks human warmth. Symbolically, this description positions Scrooge as a figure of greed and selfishness, reinforcing Dickens' criticism of capitalist excess. Emotionally, this makes the reader feel disgusted by Scrooge's behaviour and eager for his transformation.

Level Four: Explain the Effect on the Reader

Now you have:
- Answered the question in Level One
- Provided a method in Level Two
- Explained the meaning in Level Three

In Level Four, you need to analyse the effect of the method on the reader.

Use the FAULTS acronym to guide your analysis:

- **Feel – What emotions does this create?**
- **Ask – What questions does this make us ask?**
- **Understand – What does this reveal about the character or theme?**
- **Link – How does this connect to other moments in the**

text?
- **Think** – What deeper ideas does this lead us to?
- **Sympathise** – Do we relate to or judge the character?

Example of Effect on the Reader Discussion:

One of the most powerful methods Dickens uses to present Scrooge's greed is the use of semantically linked words: "tight-fisted... squeezing... grasping." Literally, these words suggest Scrooge's obsession with money—he clings to wealth as if physically unable to part with it. The verb "squeezing" connotes excessive control, as if Scrooge is wringing every last penny from those around him. Metaphorically, this highlights Scrooge's emotional poverty, as he hoards money but lacks human warmth. Symbolically, this description positions Scrooge as a figure of greed and selfishness, reinforcing Dickens' criticism of capitalist excess. Emotionally, this makes the reader feel disgusted by Scrooge's behaviour and eager for his transformation. The effect on the reader is a mixture of disgust and anticipation for Scrooge's eventual transformation. We feel frustrated with Scrooge's selfishness, but also curious to see if he can change. We ask whether greed is a choice or a product of social conditioning. We understand that Scrooge's attitude represents the widespread selfishness of the wealthy elite in Victorian society. We link this moment to his eventual redemption, showing the stark contrast between his past and future self. We think about Dickens' criticism of capitalism and the importance of generosity. We sympathise with Scrooge later in the novella when we see that his behaviour stems from a lonely childhood.

Level Five: Explain Dickens' Intention

At this stage, it may feel like you've exhausted your analysis. However, to reach the highest grades, consider Dickens' purpose in writing the novella.

Use the RECIPES acronym to explore the writer's intent:

- **Reveal** – What does Dickens reveal about society?
- **Emphasise** – What idea does he highlight?
- **Create** – What emotions does he evoke?
- **Imply** – What does this suggest about morality or human nature?
- **Portray** – How does this develop our understanding of Scrooge?
- **Exaggerate** – How does Dickens heighten the drama?
- **Steer** – What is he making us think or question?

Example of Author's Intention Discussion:

> One of the most powerful methods Dickens uses to present Scrooge's greed is the use of semantically linked words: "tight-fisted... squeezing... grasping." Literally, these words suggest Scrooge's obsession with money—he clings to wealth as if physically unable to part with it. The verb "squeezing" connotes excessive control, as if Scrooge is wringing every last penny from those around him. Metaphorically, this highlights Scrooge's emotional poverty, as he hoards money but lacks human warmth. Symbolically, this description positions Scrooge as a figure of greed and selfishness, reinforcing Dickens' criticism of capitalist excess.

Emotionally, this makes the reader feel disgusted by Scrooge's behaviour and eager for his transformation. The effect on the reader is a mixture of disgust and anticipation for Scrooge's eventual transformation. We feel frustrated with Scrooge's selfishness, but also curious to see if he can change. We ask whether greed is a choice or a product of social conditioning. We understand that Scrooge's attitude represents the widespread selfishness of the wealthy elite in Victorian society. We link this moment to his eventual redemption, showing the stark contrast between his past and future self. We think about Dickens' criticism of capitalism and the importance of generosity. We sympathise with Scrooge later in the novella when we see that his behaviour stems from a lonely childhood.

Dickens may have wanted to steer his Victorian audience towards recognising the dangers of selfishness. By exaggerating Scrooge's greed through negative adjectives and metaphors, Dickens emphasises the need for social responsibility. Scrooge's transformation from miser to philanthropist suggests that change is possible, reinforcing Dickens' message that kindness benefits all of society. Through A Christmas Carol, Dickens critiques the attitudes of the wealthy, urging his audience to embrace generosity and compassion. Dickens steers the reader towards the idea that greed isolates people, and that redemption is only possible through human connection.

Level Six: Link to Wider Text, Context, or Concept

To make your response thoughtful and perceptive, consider:
- **The wider novel – How does this moment foreshadow later events?**

- **Key concepts** – What fundamental human ideas does this explore?
- **Historical context** – How does this reflect Victorian values?

Example of Contextual Discussion:

Overall, Dickens is asking us to consider the fundamental concept of social responsibility. Within the novel, this moment contrasts with Scrooge's eventual redemption, reinforcing Dickens' belief that anyone can change. Conceptually, it links to Christian morality, as Dickens suggests that true wealth comes from generosity, not money. Historically, it reflects the harsh realities of Victorian poverty, aligning with Dickens' advocacy for social reform.

Examples:

The Power of Redemption

Quote: "I will honour Christmas in my heart, and try to keep it all the year." (Stave 4)

One of the most powerful methods Dickens uses to present redemption as transformative is the motif of the heart, seen in Scrooge's declaration, "I will honour Christmas in my heart." The noun "heart" symbolises emotions, morality, and human warmth —qualities that Scrooge previously rejected. The verb "honour" conveys a sense of deep respect and commitment, implying that Scrooge is not simply changing his actions but fundamentally altering his entire worldview.

Literally, this moment follows Scrooge's vision of his own death, where he realises that his life has been one of isolation and cruelty. Metaphorically, the phrase "keep it all the year" suggests that Christmas is not just a holiday but a state of mind—one of generosity and compassion. Symbolically, Scrooge's transformation reflects wider Victorian concerns about wealth and social responsibility, reinforcing Dickens' message that kindness should extend beyond a single season.

For the reader, this moment evokes hope and catharsis—we witness Scrooge's genuine change and feel reassured that even the most selfish individuals can find redemption. Dickens steers us towards the idea that true change requires self-reflection and action; it is not enough to regret one's past—one must actively choose to be better.

From a structural perspective, this moment marks the climax of Scrooge's redemptive arc. By using a first-person pledge, Dickens ensures that Scrooge's transformation feels personal and sincere. The novel, written in the form of a morality tale, reinforces the idea that selfishness can be unlearned, and that society benefits when individuals choose generosity over greed.

The Importance Of Family And Love

Quote: "Bob held his withered little hand in his, as if he loved the child, and wished to keep him by his side." (Stave 3)

One of the most powerful methods Dickens uses to present family as the true source of wealth is contrast, particularly between the Cratchits and Scrooge. The phrase "withered little hand" highlights Tiny Tim's frailty and vulnerability, reinforcing the Cratchit family's financial struggles. However, the verb "held" conveys warmth and tenderness, showing that Bob's love for his son is more valuable than material wealth.

Literally, this moment takes place during Scrooge's visit with the Ghost of Christmas Present, as he observes the Cratchit family celebrating Christmas despite their poverty. Metaphorically, Tiny Tim represents the consequences of social inequality—his survival depends on the generosity of others. Symbolically, Bob's gesture acts as a stark contrast to Scrooge's earlier isolation, reminding both Scrooge and the reader that true happiness is found in human connection, not financial success.

For the reader, this moment evokes sympathy and admiration—we recognise the Cratchits' hardships, but also their unwavering love for one another. Dickens steers us towards questioning Victorian attitudes toward poverty, urging readers to see the working class not as burdens, but as families with dignity and worth.

Structurally, this moment serves as a foil to Scrooge's coldness, intensifying the impact of his later redemption. By embedding Tiny Tim's fate within Scrooge's transformation, Dickens reinforces his message: without compassion, the most vulnerable in society will suffer. The Cratchits, though poor, embody the true spirit of Christmas, forcing Scrooge—and the reader—to reconsider what it truly means to be rich.

Social Responsibility And The Treatment Of The Poor

Quote: "Are there no prisons? Are there no workhouses?" (Stave 1)

One of the most powerful methods Dickens uses to critique social injustice is rhetorical questioning, particularly through Scrooge's dismissive response to the poor. The repetition of "Are there no" implies cold detachment and indifference, as if Scrooge sees the suffering of others as an administrative problem rather with Scrooge, as she sees that his priorities have shifted. Metaphorically, it represents the emotional cost of greed—Scrooge has sacrificed companionship for financial gain. Symbolically, Belle embodies what could have been, serving as a reminder that Scrooge's loneliness is self-inflicted.

For the reader, this moment evokes sadness and reflection, as we witness the defining moment that led to Scrooge's isolation. Dickens steers us towards the idea that wealth cannot replace love, reinforcing his message that personal relationships are more valuable than financial success.

Structurally, this moment is crucial in Scrooge's emotional journey. The Ghost of Christmas Past forces him to confront his mistakes, suggesting that memory has the power to bring about change. Dickens, writing in a time when industrialisation often prioritised profit over people, uses this moment to critique the idea that success is measured by wealth alone.

The Fragility Of Life

Quote: "If he be like to die, he had better do it, and decrease the surplus population." (Stave 1)

One of the most powerful methods Dickens uses to expose cruelty towards the poor is irony, particularly in the repetition of Scrooge's own words later in the novel. The verb "decrease" dehumanises the poor, treating them as mere statistics rather than individuals. The noun "surplus" suggests that those who are weak or struggling are an economic burden, reflecting the brutal attitudes of the upper class.

Literally, Scrooge says this to justify his refusal to donate to charity. Metaphorically, it represents the mindset that values productivity over human dignity—Tiny Tim's life is worth less because he cannot contribute financially. Symbolically, this line serves as a moral reckoning—when Scrooge later begs for Tiny Tim's survival, he is forced to confront the cruelty of his former self.

For the reader, this moment evokes outrage and shame, as Dickens forces us to consider how society treats its most vulnerable. He steers us towards rejecting Malthusian economics, which suggested that poverty was necessary to control population growth.

Structurally, this moment is part of Scrooge's self-confrontation. The repetition of his own words later in the novel highlights his transformation, reinforcing Dickens' belief that personal change is possible when we choose empathy over greed.

Fate And Free Will

Quote: "The Spirits of all Three shall strive within me." (Stave 5)

One of the most powerful methods Dickens uses to explore fate and free will is personification, particularly in Scrooge's description of the ghosts as forces that exist within him. The verb "strive" suggests inner conflict, implying that Scrooge is actively choosing to carry their lessons forward rather than passively receiving them. The noun "Spirits" not only refers to the ghosts but also to the moral messages they represent—past regret, present responsibility, and future consequence.

Literally, this moment marks Scrooge's redemption, as he pledges to change. Metaphorically, it suggests that personal growth is an ongoing struggle—transformation does not happen instantly but requires conscious effort. Symbolically, it reinforces the novel's

Christian message: salvation is possible for all, but only if they acknowledge their sins and work towards redemption.

For the reader, this moment evokes relief and hope, as we see that Scrooge's change is sincere. Dickens steers us towards the idea that while fate may guide us, it is our choices that define us, reinforcing the novel's central moral lesson.

Structurally, this moment serves as the resolution of the novel's moral arc. The ghosts, though supernatural, are ultimately a means of self-discovery, emphasising that the power to change lies within Scrooge himself. By ending with an image of active transformation, Dickens ensures that the novel's message of generosity and kindness lingers long after the final page.

EXTEND - UNIVERSAL CONCEPTS IN A CHRISTMAS CAROL

This chapter provides you with some thinking points relating to the universal concepts we looked at earlier, specifically for A Christmas Carol. You can use these as revision by asking people to test you on your ability to think of relevant examples of each concept, as well as those listed here.

Freedom and Restriction

Example 1: Marley's Chains – Marley is literally bound by the chains he forged in life, symbolising the consequences of his greed and selfishness. He is trapped in eternal suffering, warning Scrooge that his current lifestyle will lead to the same fate.

Example 2: Scrooge's Emotional Imprisonment – Scrooge restricts himself from joy, love, and human connection. His obsession with money isolates him, showing that self-imposed restriction can be just as damaging as physical chains.

Innocence and Corruption

Example 1: Tiny Tim's Purity – Tiny Tim embodies innocence, hope, and goodness, despite his suffering. His unwavering optimism contrasts with Scrooge's cynicism, showing the resilience of innocence.

Example 2: Ignorance and Want – These ghostly children personify societal corruption. Their presence warns that if society continues to neglect the poor, ignorance will breed destruction and Want will lead to despair.

Dreams and Reality

Example 1: Scrooge's Visions – The ghostly visits blur the lines between dreams and reality. The spirits force Scrooge to confront hard truths, making him realise that his current life choices will lead to a lonely, forgotten death.

Example 2: Scrooge's Future Grave – The vision of Scrooge's neglected grave symbolises the stark reality of his fate. The fear it instils in him forces him to change, showing the power of confronting harsh truths.

Love and Hate

Example 1: Fezziwig's Warmth vs. Scrooge's Coldness – Fezziwig, as a kind-hearted employer, represents love and generosity, while Scrooge, before his transformation, represents greed and emotional coldness.

Example 2: Fred's Love vs. Scrooge's Detachment – Fred's persistent invitations to Christmas dinner contrast with Scrooge's rejection of family. Scrooge's eventual change highlights the redemptive power of love.

Safety and Danger

Example 1: The Cratchits' Fragile Security – Bob Cratchit's family represents the precariousness of poverty. They find safety in their love and unity, but the threat of Tiny Tim's death looms over them.

Example 2: Scrooge's Isolation – At the start, Scrooge believes safety lies in financial security. However, by the end, he realises that emotional and social isolation is far more dangerous.

Truth and Lies

Example 1: Scrooge's Perception of Himself – At first, Scrooge lies to himself, believing he is practical rather than miserly. The spirits force him to see the truth of his actions and their consequences.

Example 2: The Ghost of Christmas Yet to Come – The silent, faceless ghost symbolises the unknown future, revealing an unavoidable truth: if Scrooge does not change, he will be forgotten and despised.

Universal Relationships in *A Christmas Carol*

Young and Old

Example 1: Scrooge's Past vs. Present Self – The Ghost of Christmas Past shows Scrooge as a lonely, neglected child, contrasting with his current hardened, cynical self.

Example 2: Tiny Tim and Scrooge's Redemption – Tiny Tim, a symbol of youthful innocence and vulnerability, plays a key role in Scrooge's transformation, inspiring him to act with kindness.

Rich and Poor

Example 1: Scrooge vs. the Cratchits – Scrooge has wealth but lacks love and joy, while the Cratchits have little money but abundant warmth and happiness.

Example 2: The Charity Collectors – Their request for donations highlights the vast divide between the wealthy and the struggling poor in Victorian society.

Leader and Follower

Example 1: Fezziwig as a Benevolent Leader – He treats his employees with kindness, showing that leadership can be both profitable and compassionate.

Example 2: Scrooge's Influence Over Bob Cratchit – Bob is completely at Scrooge's mercy, yet he remains loyal and kind. This contrast highlights the power imbalance between employer and employee.

Lost and Found

Example 1: Scrooge's Lost Love – His fiancée, Belle, leaves him because he prioritises wealth over love. His chance for happiness is lost due to his greed.

Example 2: Scrooge's Redemption – He finds joy and purpose again when he reconnects with humanity, making amends with Fred and helping the Cratchits.

Effort and Reward

Example 1: The Cratchits' Hard Work – Despite their struggles, the Cratchits' perseverance is rewarded through love, family, and, eventually, Scrooge's generosity.

Example 2: Scrooge's Redemption – His transformation requires emotional effort, but the reward is a life of joy, connection, and second chances.

Endings and Beginnings

Example 1: Marley's Death vs. Scrooge's Future – Marley's death represents a tragic ending without redemption, *serving as a warning for Scrooge's own possible fate.*

Example 2: Scrooge's Christmas Morning Transformation – The final chapter marks a new beginning for Scrooge, symbolising rebirth and hope.

Nature and Man

Example 1: Cold Weather as a Symbol of Scrooge's Heart – The icy winter reflects Scrooge's cold and unfeeling nature.

Example 2: The Warmth of the Cratchit Home – Despite the harsh winter, their home is filled with warmth, contrasting with Scrooge's cold, empty house.

Universal Fears in A Christmas Carol

Loss

Example 1: Scrooge's Lost Childhood Joy – His past self was full of love and hope, but he lost that part of himself through greed.

Example 2: The Cratchits' Fear of Losing Tiny Tim – The possible death of Tiny Tim represents the real-life consequences of poverty and neglect.

Death

Example 1: Marley's Ghost – Marley's fate after death

serves as a grim warning about the consequences of a selfish life.

Example 2: Scrooge's Future Grave – The image of Scrooge's own unvisited grave forces him to confront his mortality and its meaning.

Money

Example 1: Scrooge's Obsession with Wealth – He prioritises money over human connection, ultimately leaving him isolated and unloved.

Example 2: The Thieves Ransacking Scrooge's Possessions – In the vision of his future, Scrooge sees that his wealth does not bring him respect or mourning, only greed from others.

Isolation

Example 1: Scrooge's Self-Imposed Loneliness – He refuses social interaction and rejects kindness, believing money is more valuable than relationships.

Example 2: Scrooge's Future Fate – The vision of his solitary death reveals the ultimate consequence of his isolation.

Abandonment

Example 1: Young Scrooge Left Alone at School – The Ghost of Christmas Past shows his childhood loneliness, which shaped his later distrust of others.

Example 2: Belle Leaving Scrooge – Her decision to end their engagement highlights how his love for money cost him personal happiness.

Disenfranchisement

Example 1: The Poor in Victorian Society – The charity collectors and Cratchits represent those ignored and abandoned by a society focused on wealth.

Example 2: Ignorance and Want – The two children personify the neglect and suffering of the lower classes, warning of the dangers of social inequality.

EXTEND - HISTORICAL CONTEXT

The following chapter gives you some ideas about how to link the historical context of the novel with Dickens's methods and the universal concepts. These ideas canbe used by you as plans for your own thesis statements.

The Industrial Revolution → Rich And Poor → Symbolism Of Scrooge's House

Context: The rapid industrialisation of Britain led to extreme wealth disparities, with factory owners growing rich while workers lived in poverty.
Concept: Dickens contrasts Scrooge's wealth with the suffering of the poor, showing that financial success without generosity leads to isolation.
Method: Symbolism in the description of Scrooge's house.
Example: "Darkness is cheap, and Scrooge liked it." (Stave 1)
Effect: The darkness symbolises Scrooge's self-imposed isolation, showing how greed leads to a lack of warmth—both literal and emotional.

The Poor Law And Workhouses → Freedom And Restriction → Rhetorical Questions

Context: Harsh workhouses and the Poor Law Amendment Act of 1834 forced the unemployed into dreadful conditions, stripping them of dignity.

Concept: Scrooge embodies the societal view that poverty is the fault of the poor, which Dickens critiques.
Method: Rhetorical questions in Scrooge's response to charity collectors.
Example: "Are there no prisons? Are there no workhouses?" (Stave 1)
Effect: Scrooge's dismissive tone mirrors Victorian attitudes towards poverty, making Dickens' readers question whether wealth should equate to moral superiority.

Victorian Christmas Traditions → Endings And Beginnings → Contrast In Atmosphere

Context: Christmas was becoming a more family-centred, charitable holiday during the Victorian era, largely influenced by A Christmas Carol itself.
Concept: Scrooge begins by rejecting Christmas but transforms into a figure of joy and generosity.
Method: Contrast in atmosphere between Stave 1 and Stave 5.
Example: "I am as light as a feather, I am as happy as an angel, I am as merry as a schoolboy." (Stave 5)
Effect: The uplifting imagery in Stave 5 contrasts with the cold bleakness of Stave 1, reinforcing Scrooge's redemption.

Malthusian Economics → Safety And Danger → Metaphor Of The 'Ignorance' And 'Want' Children

Context: Economist Thomas Malthus argued that poverty was inevitable due to overpopulation and limited resources, justifying lack of charity.
Concept: Dickens warns that ignoring social injustice will lead to society's ruin.
Method: Metaphor in the personification of Ignorance and Want.
Example: "This boy is Ignorance. This girl is Want. Beware them both." (Stave 3)

Effect: The children symbolise the dangers of neglecting education and welfare, showing that societal issues must be addressed to prevent catastrophe.

Victorian Attitudes Towards The Supernatural → Truth And Lies → Hyperbolic Description Of Marley's Ghost

Context: Ghost stories were a popular tradition, particularly at Christmas, and Victorians were fascinated by spiritualism.
Concept: Scrooge initially denies the existence of ghosts, reflecting his rejection of moral truths.
Method: Hyperbole in Marley's ghostly presence.
Example: "I wear the chain I forged in life." (Stave 1)
Effect: The exaggerated imagery of Marley's chains reinforces the idea that past actions leave permanent consequences, forcing Scrooge to confront his own future.

The Power Of Redemption → Innocence And Corruption → Pathetic Fallacy

Context: The Victorian era was heavily influenced by Christian morality, promoting redemption through good deeds.
Concept: Scrooge begins as a symbol of corruption but finds innocence again through his transformation.
Method: Pathetic fallacy in the weather.
Example: "No fog, no mist; clear, bright, jovial, stirring cold." (Stave 5)
Effect: The contrast in weather between the opening and closing staves mirrors Scrooge's internal change, with the clear skies symbolising newfound clarity.

The Treatment Of The Poor → Love And Hate → Repetition In Fred's Dialogue

Context: Middle-class Victorians often viewed the poor as lazy or

undeserving, an idea Dickens challenges.
Concept: Fred represents unconditional love and goodwill, which Scrooge initially rejects.
Method: Repetition in Fred's speech about Christmas.
Example: "A kind, forgiving, charitable, pleasant time." (Stave 1)
Effect: The listing and repetition of positive adjectives contrast with Scrooge's coldness, reinforcing Christmas as a time of generosity and unity.

Family And Generational Wealth → Young And Old → Symbolism Of The Cratchit Family Meal

Context: In Victorian society, wealth was often passed down, but hard-working families like the Cratchits had no financial security.
Concept: Dickens highlights the struggles of honest, hardworking people versus the selfishness of the rich.
Method: Symbolism in the Christmas dinner scene.
Example: "There never was such a goose." (Stave 3)
Effect: The Cratchits' joy over their small meal symbolises resilience and the idea that love, not money, defines a family's worth.

The Fear Of A Lonely Death → Loss → Foreshadowing And Irony In Scrooge's Tombstone

Context: Victorians placed great importance on legacy, yet Dickens warns that a selfish life leads to being forgotten.
Concept: Scrooge's future shows the ultimate consequence of his isolation—his death means nothing to anyone.
Method: Foreshadowing and irony in the vision of his grave.
Example: "It was a worthy place. Walled in by houses; overrun by grass and weeds." (Stave 4)
Effect: The neglected grave foreshadows Scrooge's fate if he does not change, forcing both him and the reader to reflect on the value of a meaningful life.

The Celebration Of Community → Isolation → Contrast In Dialogue Between Scrooge And Bob Cratchit

Context: The importance of community and festive spirit was growing in Victorian England, but many, like Scrooge, rejected it.

Concept: Scrooge isolates himself, while the Cratchits and Fred thrive in companionship.

Method: Contrast in tone and dialogue.

Example: Scrooge: "If they would rather die, they had better do it, and decrease the surplus population." (Stave 1) Bob Cratchit: "I'll give you Mr Scrooge, the Founder of the Feast." (Stave 3)

Effect: The contrast between Scrooge's callous statement and Bob's gratitude highlights the difference between selfishness and generosity, reinforcing the novella's message that kindness enriches life.

EXTEND - DICKENS' METHODS

1. Allegory – The Entire Story as a Moral Lesson

Example: Scrooge is visited by three spirits who force him to confront his past, present, and future.

Explanation: The structure of A Christmas Carol functions as an allegory, with each ghost symbolising a stage in moral enlightenment. The novella presents a journey of transformation, with Scrooge moving from selfishness to generosity.

Link to Universal Concepts: Endings and Beginnings – The novella shows how change is possible, no matter how ingrained someone's faults are.

Link to Scrooge's Journey: Scrooge starts as miserly and cruel, but by the end, he is reborn into a compassionate figure, proving that redemption is always within reach.

2. Pathetic Fallacy – The Weather Reflecting Scrooge's Character

Example: "It was cold, bleak, biting weather: foggy withal." (Stave 1)

Explanation: Dickens uses pathetic fallacy to reflect Scrooge's cold-hearted nature. The harsh winter setting mirrors Scrooge's lack of empathy and isolation.

Link to Universal Concepts: Isolation and Disenfranchisement – Scrooge has cut himself off from human connection, much like the cold fog isolates the city.

Link to Scrooge's Journey: At the beginning, Scrooge is emotionally frozen, but by the end, the weather imagery softens, reflecting his warming heart.

3. Symbolism – Marley's Chains as the Burden of Greed

Example: "I wear the chain I forged in life." (Stave 1)

Explanation: Marley's chains represent his past sins—they are a physical manifestation of his greed and selfishness. Dickens warns the reader that wealth without kindness leads to suffering.

Link to Universal Concepts: Money and Morality – Marley's suffering reminds us that wealth alone does not bring happiness.

Link to Scrooge's Journey: This moment shocks Scrooge, planting the first seed of fear that he too may suffer the same fate if he does not change.

4. Foreshadowing – Tiny Tim's Possible Death

Example: "If these shadows remain unaltered by the Future, the child will die." (Stave 3)

Explanation: The Ghost of Christmas Present warns that Tiny Tim's fate is not fixed—his survival depends on whether society, and Scrooge, change their ways. This foreshadowing intensifies Scrooge's guilt and moral awakening.

Link to Universal Concepts: Life and Death – Dickens explores how poverty directly leads to suffering, particularly for the vulnerable.

Link to Scrooge's Journey: This moment deepens Scrooge's fear and remorse, making him realise the consequences of his inaction.

5. Characterisation – The Cratchit Family as a Symbol of Joy in Poverty

Example: "They were happy, grateful, pleased with one another, and contented with the time." (Stave 3)

Explanation: Despite their poverty, the Cratchits are full of love and gratitude. Dickens contrasts their warmth and unity with Scrooge's loneliness, emphasising that wealth does not determine happiness.

Link to Universal Concepts: Rich and Poor – The Cratchits prove that human connection is more valuable than money.

Link to Scrooge's Journey: Seeing the Cratchits' joy despite hardship forces Scrooge to reconsider his view of wealth and generosity.

6. Juxtaposition – Fezziwig vs. Scrooge as Employers

Example: "The happiness he gives, is quite as great as if it cost a fortune." (Stave 2)

Explanation: Fezziwig is presented as a benevolent employer, providing joy and community, while Scrooge exploits his workers. Dickens highlights the impact of kindness in leadership.

Link to Universal Concepts: Effort and Reward – Fezziwig shows that investing in others brings lasting joy, unlike Scrooge, who hoards wealth but remains miserable.

Link to Scrooge's Journey: Fezziwig serves as a contrast and a lost ideal, making Scrooge realise what he could have been.

7. Irony – Scrooge's Own Words Used Against Him

Example: "If he be like to die, he had better do it, and decrease the surplus population." (Stave 3)

Explanation: The Ghost of Christmas Present throws Scrooge's earlier words back at him, forcing him to confront his own cruelty. This irony shames him and marks a significant step in his transformation.

Link to Universal Concepts: Truth and Lies – Scrooge realises that his beliefs about the poor were lies he told himself to justify his selfishness.

Link to Scrooge's Journey: This is a key turning point, as Scrooge begins to truly regret his past attitudes.

8. Gothic Imagery – The Ghost of Christmas Yet to Come

Example: "It was shrouded in a deep black garment, which concealed its head, its face, its form." (Stave 4)

Explanation: The Ghost of Christmas Yet to Come is terrifyingly vague, representing the unknown and inevitable nature of death.

Link to Universal Concepts: Fear of the Unknown – The ghost's mystery forces Scrooge to confront his mortality.

Link to Scrooge's Journey: This encounter is the climax of Scrooge's transformation, as he realises the horror of dying unloved and unmourned.

9. Contrast – Scrooge's Grave vs. Tiny Tim's Death

Example: "A churchyard, overrun by grass and weeds, the growth of vegetation's death, not life." (Stave 4)

Explanation: Scrooge's uncared-for grave contrasts sharply with Tiny Tim's mourned and remembered death, showing that a selfish life leads to a forgotten death.

Link to Universal Concepts: Legacy and Remembrance – Dickens asks us: How do we want to be remembered?

Link to Scrooge's Journey: Scrooge's final horror at seeing his grave compels him to embrace change wholeheartedly.

10. Transformation – Scrooge's Complete Redemption

Example: "I will honour Christmas in my heart, and try to keep it all the year." (Stave 5)

Explanation: The final act of Scrooge's transformation sees him embracing kindness, generosity, and human connection.

Link to Universal Concepts: Endings and New Beginnings – Scrooge proves that change is always possible.

Link to Scrooge's Journey: He has gone from selfish and lonely to joyful and loved, proving Dickens' message that everyone has the power to change for the better.

EXTEND - STRUCTURAL DECISIONS IN A CHRISTMAS CAROL

Dickens carefully constructs the structure of A Christmas Carol to reinforce its themes of redemption, morality, and social responsibility. The novella's pacing, division, narrative techniques, and contrasts all serve to emphasise the transformative journey of Scrooge. Below is a breakdown of Dickens' key structural choices, their effects, and how they link to universal concepts.

1. The Five-Stave Structure – A Moral Allegory in a Christmas Setting

What is it?

Instead of chapters, A Christmas Carol is divided into five "staves", reinforcing the idea of a carol (song) with separate verses. This structure creates a rhythmic, musical quality and reflects the joyful spirit of the season.

Why does Dickens do this?

Creates a cyclical structure – The novella begins and ends with Christmas, symbolising a complete transformation.

Mimics traditional oral storytelling – Enhances its moral, fairy-tale-like quality, making it more accessible to all readers.

Suggests a lesson to be learned – The five-part structure mirrors a journey through sin, recognition, redemption, and renewal.

Link to Universal Concepts:

Endings and Beginnings – Scrooge's character returns to where he started, but as a changed man.

Truth and Lies – Each stave forces Scrooge to confront a different aspect of his past deceptions and eventual truth.

Structural Effect on the Reader:

The five-stave structure makes the novel feel like a fable or moral parable, ensuring its message is easily remembered and retold.

2. The Use of Time – A Condensed and Intensified Transformation

What is it?

The entire narrative takes place over one night, creating a sense of urgency. Scrooge must witness, understand, and change within a single Christmas Eve, mirroring the fleeting chance humans have to change before it is too late.

Why does Dickens do this?

Compresses time to heighten drama – Scrooge's rapid transformation feels miraculous, emphasising that change is always possible.

Reinforces the supernatural tone – The spirits manipulate time, showing Scrooge events from past, present, and future in quick succession.

Creates a sense of inevitability – The fast-paced structure mirrors the relentless march toward death, redemption, or damnation.

Link to Universal Concepts:

Death – Time is running out for Scrooge. The Ghost of Christmas Yet to Come symbolises that all paths lead to death, but how we are remembered is within our control.

Lost and Found – Scrooge has "lost" his past self, but finds it again through this condensed, supernatural intervention.

Structural Effect on the Reader:

The fast-moving timeline makes Scrooge's revelations feel immediate and powerful, urging the reader to consider their own time-limited choices.

3. The Framing Device – Scrooge's Journey as a Morality Tale

What is it?

Dickens frames the novel around Scrooge's journey, opening with his self-imposed isolation and ending with his rejoining of society. This clear structural progression mirrors a religious or moral lesson.

Why does Dickens do this?

Encourages self-reflection – The reader witnesses Scrooge's moral fall and rise, making them reflect on their own actions.

Creates a fable-like simplicity – The direct, structured storytelling makes the message clear and universal.

Makes Scrooge a surrogate for the reader – Dickens guides the audience through his transformation, making them question whether they, too, need redemption.

Link to Universal Concepts:

Isolation and Reconnection – Scrooge's physical and emotional isolation at the start is completely reversed by the end.

Effort and Reward – The structure shows that change is difficult but leads to immense joy.

Structural Effect on the Reader:

By mirroring a religious parable or fable, Dickens ensures that the reader engages with the novel as both a story and a lesson.

4. The Ghosts as Structural Divisions – Past, Present, and Future

What is it?

Each ghost represents a key stage of Scrooge's development. Dickens structures the novella into three clear "lessons", ensuring the transformation feels progressive and inevitable.

Why does Dickens do this?

Symbolises personal reflection – The ghosts force Scrooge to evaluate his life in three distinct ways: Past: What shaped him? Present: What is he doing wrong now? Future: What will happen if he doesn't change?

Increases narrative tension – The spirits become increasingly more serious and intense, heightening Scrooge's fear and desperation.

Link to Universal Concepts:

Dreams and Reality – Scrooge lives in denial, but the ghosts force him to see the truth.

Love and Hate – The contrast between past love (Belle) and present greed shows how his emotions shaped his downfall.

Structural Effect on the Reader:

By giving Scrooge three distinct "chances" to understand himself,

Dickens makes his redemption feel earned and convincing.

5. Circular Structure – Returning to the Beginning but Changed

What is it?

The novel begins and ends with Scrooge at Christmas, but the tone and atmosphere completely change.

Why does Dickens do this?

Shows total transformation – Scrooge begins in darkness and ends in light.

Emphasises the power of choice – He is given the same situation (Christmas Day) but responds differently, proving that change is possible for everyone.

Link to Universal Concepts:

Endings and Beginnings – A literal "new beginning" for Scrooge, proving that redemption can happen at any point in life.

Money and Morality – Dickens contrasts Scrooge's former greed with his new generosity, proving that wealth does not define character.

Structural Effect on the Reader:

The circular structure makes the reader appreciate how far

Scrooge has come, reinforcing Dickens' message that self-improvement is within everyone's reach.

Gap-Fill Exercises for Structural Analysis in *A Christmas Carol*

Below are **three gap-fill exercises** to help you engage with Dickens' structural decisions. Each one increases in complexity. Fill in the blanks with your own interpretations and analysis.

Gap-Fill 1: The Five-Stave Structure *(Basic Level)*

One of the most powerful structural choices Dickens makes is the _____ structure of the novella, where instead of chapters, he divides the story into five "_____." This mirrors the form of a _____, reinforcing the novel's _____ tone.

The structure creates a sense of _____, as the novella begins and ends with Scrooge on _____. However, by the end, he has completely _____. This cyclical structure emphasises the theme of _____, showing that personal transformation is always possible.

Through this, Dickens may be _____ his readers towards the idea that Christmas is not just a day, but a _____ for how people should live all year round.

Gap-Fill 2: The Use of Time and the Supernatural *(Intermediate Level)*

Dickens condenses Scrooge's transformation into a single _____, which creates a sense of _____ and intensifies the novella's message. The visits from the three spirits take Scrooge through _____, _____, and _____, forcing him to confront the consequences of his actions.

One of the most powerful methods Dickens uses is the manipulation of _____. The Ghost of Christmas _____ shows Scrooge visions of his youth, reminding him of his former innocence and lost _____. The Ghost of Christmas _____ presents Scrooge with the harsh realities of his current choices, particularly through the characters of _____ and _____. Finally, the Ghost of Christmas _____ presents a terrifying, wordless vision of _____, where Scrooge sees his own _____.

By the end of the novella, Dickens presents time as something that can be _____, but only if one chooses to change before it is too late.

This structural choice may suggest that Dickens wants the reader to consider _____, asking them whether they will choose to change their ways like Scrooge or face the same _____.

Gap-Fill 3: The Circular Narrative and Redemption *(Advanced Level)*

Dickens structures *A Christmas Carol* in a circular way, beginning and ending on _____, with Scrooge as the central focus. However, the contrast between the two Christmases highlights his _____.

At the start of the novel, Scrooge is described as "solitary as _____," symbolising his complete isolation. The first stave depicts him rejecting the festive spirit by _____. In contrast, by the end of the novella, Scrooge is described as "as good a _____ as the good old city knew," reflecting his transformation.

One of the most powerful methods Dickens uses to emphasise this change is the contrast in _____. Early in the novel, Scrooge's speech is cold and dismissive, as seen in his infamous phrase, _____. However, in the final stave, his tone is filled with _____, seen in his interactions with Bob Cratchit and Tiny Tim.

This circular structure reinforces the theme of _____. Dickens may be suggesting that change is always _____, and that no matter how miserly or selfish someone is, they can still choose to _____.

Through this, Dickens steers the reader towards considering their own _____ and how they treat those around them, particularly during _____.

PRACTISE - GAP-FILL EXERCISES

Gap-Fill 1: Scrooge's Transformation (Simple)

Instructions: Fill in the blanks using the **word bank** at the bottom. At the start of *A Christmas Carol*, Dickens presents Scrooge as a **(1)** _____ and **(2)** _____ man who values money above people. This reflects Victorian society's focus on **(3)** _____, where the rich believed the poor were responsible for their own suffering. Scrooge's dismissive attitude is shown when he refuses to give to charity, asking, **(4) "Are there no** _____**?"**
However, by the end of the novella, Scrooge is transformed. Dickens uses **(5)** _____ to contrast his past and present self, as seen in Scrooge's **(6)** _____ when he wakes up on Christmas morning and declares, **(7) "I am as light as a** _____**, I am as happy as an angel!"** This joyful language highlights his **(8)** _____, emphasising Dickens' message that **(9)** _____ and generosity are more valuable than wealth.

Word Bank:
- Money
- Metaphor
- Workhouses
- Redemption
- Greedy

- Cold-hearted
- Transformation
- Schoolboy
- Responsibility

Challenge Question: Why does Dickens make Scrooge's transformation so extreme?

Gap-Fill 2: The Role of the Ghosts (Intermediate)

Instructions: Fill in the blanks using the **word bank** at the bottom. Dickens uses the three **(1)** _____ to guide Scrooge through a journey of **(2)** _____ and self-reflection. The **(3)** _____ Ghost of Christmas Past symbolises memory, showing Scrooge key moments from his childhood, including his time at **(4)** _____, which helps the audience understand why Scrooge became so isolated. Dickens describes the ghost as **(5) "a strange figure—like a child: yet not so like a child as like an old man"**, using **(6)** _____ to show how the past exists beyond time. The Ghost of Christmas **(7)** _____ introduces Scrooge to the Cratchit family, where Dickens highlights the struggles of the **(8)** _____. Tiny Tim, despite his suffering, remains **(9)** _____, symbolising the innocence of the poor. The ghost's warning, **(10) "If these shadows remain unaltered by the Future, the child will die"**, presents Scrooge with a moral choice—continue his selfish ways or change his future.

Word Bank:
- Ignorance and Want
- Allegory
- Future
- Spirits
- Transformation
- School
- Compassionate
- Present

- Poor

Challenge Question: Why do you think Dickens chose supernatural figures rather than real people to guide Scrooge's journey?

Gap-Fill 3: Social Responsibility and the Poor (Advanced)

Instructions: Fill in the blanks using the **word bank** at the bottom. One of the key messages of *A Christmas Carol* is the importance of **(1)** _____. In Victorian England, the **(2)** _____ created extreme wealth inequality, leaving many poor while a small number of industrialists grew rich. Dickens critiques this social divide through the **(3)** _____ of the Cratchit family, who, despite their struggles, remain warm and loving.

In Stave 1, Scrooge represents the **(4)** _____ viewpoint, dismissing charity with the infamous statement, **(5) "If they would rather die, they had better do it, and decrease the surplus population."** Here, Dickens references the ideas of **(6)** _____, a theory suggesting that the poor should not be helped because their suffering was inevitable.

However, the **(7)** _____ of *Ignorance and Want* in Stave 3 directly challenges this belief. The two children, described as **(8) "yellow, meagre, ragged, scowling, wolfish"**, embody the consequences of society's neglect. Dickens uses these figures to evoke **(9)** _____, forcing both Scrooge and the reader to acknowledge their **(10)** _____ to help those in need.

Word Bank:
- Personification
- Industrial Revolution
- Malthusianism
- Social responsibility
- Symbolism
- Sympathy
- Poor

- Wealthy
- Allegory
- Responsibility

Challenge Question:
Why do you think Dickens used ghosts to convey social criticism instead of simply having characters discuss these issues directly?

Gap-Fill 4 - Exercise on Context, Concept, and Method
Instructions:

Complete the paragraph below by filling in the missing words using the **word bank** at the bottom.

Gap-Fill Paragraph:
In *A Christmas Carol*, Dickens explores the theme of **(1)** _____ and _____ through the contrast between wealth and poverty. In Victorian England, the **(2)** _____ **Revolution** created extreme social divisions, leaving many in poverty while industrialists accumulated vast fortunes. Dickens criticises this disparity through **(3)** _____ in his description of Scrooge's home, where "darkness is cheap, and Scrooge liked it." Here, the **(4)** _____ of "darkness" highlights Scrooge's miserliness and emotional isolation, reinforcing the idea that wealth without generosity leads to **(5)** _____.

By the end of the novella, Dickens presents an alternative perspective on wealth and morality. The **(6)** _____ in Stave 5 contrasts sharply with the cold, bleak tone of Stave 1. Scrooge now shares his fortune, symbolising his **(7)** _____, which aligns with the emerging Victorian emphasis on **(8)** _____ and Christmas charity.

Word Bank:
- Freedom and Restriction
- Rich and Poor
- Industrial

- Isolation
- Symbolism
- Darkness
- Redemption
- Warmth
- Generosity

PRACTISE - ANALYSE LANGUAGE STEP-BY-STEP

Method Activities – A Christmas Carol

Activity 1: Scrooge's Coldness (Beginner)

Objective: Analyse how Dickens introduces Scrooge's character through imagery.

Quote:
"No warmth could warm, nor wintry weather chill him." (Stave 1)

Task:
1. **Identify the method:** What literary technique is used?
2. **Literal meaning:** What is Dickens saying about Scrooge's personality?
3. **Symbolic meaning:** How does this connect to the novel's themes?
4. **Effect on the reader:** How do we perceive Scrooge?
5. **Link to the wider novel:** How does this foreshadow Scrooge's transformation?

Write a PASS paragraph analysing how Dickens presents Scrooge

as cold and isolated.

Activity 2: Marley's Warning (Intermediate)

Objective: Explore how Marley's ghost serves as a warning.

Quote:
"I wear the chain I forged in life." (Stave 1)

Task:
- **Identify the method:** How does Dickens use metaphor?
- **Explain meaning:** What does the "chain" represent?
- **Effect on the reader:** How does this create fear or sympathy?
- **Link to themes:** How does this connect to responsibility and redemption?

Write a PASS paragraph analysing Marley's role as a warning figure.

Activity 3: The Ghost of Christmas Present (Advanced)

Objective: Examine how Dickens critiques social inequality.

Quote:
"This boy is Ignorance. This girl is Want. Beware them both." (Stave 3)

Task:
- **Identify the method:** What does Dickens personify here?
- **Explain meaning:** Why are these children symbolic?
- **Effect on the reader:** How does this create guilt or urgency?
- **Link to the wider novel:** How does this reinforce Dickens' message on poverty?

Write a PASS paragraph analysing how Dickens presents social responsibility.

Activity 4: Tiny Tim's Fate (Advanced)

Objective: Explore how Dickens uses sympathy to drive change.

Quote:
"If these shadows remain unaltered by the Future, the child will die." (Stave 3)

Task:
- **Answer in brief:** What does this reveal about Tiny Tim's fate?
- **Identify the method:** How does Dickens use conditional language?
- **Explain meaning:** What does this teach Scrooge?
- **Effect on the reader:** How does this evoke sympathy?

Write a PASS paragraph analysing how Dickens uses Tiny Tim to highlight the consequences of neglect.

Activity 5: The Ghost of Christmas Yet to Come (Advanced)
Objective: Analyze how Dickens uses fear to encourage transformation.

Quote:
"The Spirit neither spoke nor moved." (Stave 4)

Task:
- **Identify the method:** How does silence create tension?
- **Explain meaning:** Why is this ghost different from the others?
- **Effect on the reader:** How does this build suspense?
- **Link to themes:** How does this moment highlight fate vs. free will?

Write a PASS paragraph analysing how Dickens presents Scrooge's fear of the future.

REVISION - THESIS BUILDING QUESTIONS

Instructions:
Answer these **guiding questions** to help develop your own ideas about how Dickens links context, concepts, and methods.

1. **Scrooge's House as Symbolism**
   - What kind of imagery does Dickens use to describe Scrooge's house in Stave 1?
   - How does the description of his house reflect his personality?
   - By the end of the novella, has this symbolism changed? How?

2. **Rhetorical Questions and Workhouses**
   - Why does Scrooge respond to the charity collectors with rhetorical questions?
   - What does this reveal about Victorian attitudes towards poverty?
   - How does Scrooge's attitude change by the end?

3. **Foreshadowing in Scrooge's Tombstone**
   - How does Dickens describe Scrooge's gravestone?
   - Why does Scrooge react so fearfully when he sees it?
   - What message might Dickens be sending to his audience about legacy and change?

4. **The Contrast Between Stave 1 and Stave 5**
   - How does Dickens describe the setting and

atmosphere at the beginning of the novella?
- How does this shift in the final stave?
- What does this contrast show about the transformation of Scrooge's character?

REVISION - EXAMPLE ESSAYS

These essays offer the basis for a strong piece of your own. The thesis is complete but the analytical paragraphs have room for improvement.

Use them to practice implementing the PASS method more thoroughly; rewrite the analysis to reflect what this book has taught you.

Essay 1: How does Dickens present the theme of redemption in *A Christmas Carol*?

Thesis Statement
In *A Christmas Carol*, Dickens takes us on a journey of understanding, exploring the idea that redemption is possible for even the most hardened individuals. He presents Scrooge as a character who begins as a symbol of greed and selfishness, yet through supernatural intervention and self-reflection, he transforms into a figure of generosity and joy. The conflict between personal greed and social responsibility is central to Scrooge's journey, as his initial resistance to change is met with increasingly powerful visions that force him to confront the consequences of his actions. By the end of the novella, Dickens has steered us towards the idea that redemption is not only possible but essential for both personal fulfilment and societal well-being.

One of the most powerful methods Dickens uses to present this transformation is **characterisation**, showing Scrooge's dramatic evolution through his actions, dialogue, and interactions with the ghosts.

PASS Paragraph
Dickens presents redemption as both a personal choice and a moral necessity, using **characterisation** to emphasise Scrooge's dramatic transformation. At the start of the novella, Scrooge is described through a series of harsh adjectives: *"tight-fisted hand at the grindstone... a squeezing, wrenching, grasping, scraping, clutching, covetous old sinner!"* The repeated verbs of **grasping** and **clutching** connote his obsessive greed, as though he is physically clinging onto his wealth. However, by the end of the novella, Scrooge's dialogue has shifted dramatically; he exclaims, *"I am as light as a feather, I am as happy as an angel!"* The use of similes presents his **emotional rebirth**, contrasting his previous weighty burdens with newfound freedom. The shift in Scrooge's character is not just personal but symbolic; he moves from being a representation of capitalist greed to embodying Dickens' ideal of social responsibility. This transformation would have resonated with a Victorian audience, many of whom were grappling with the consequences of industrialisation and poverty. Dickens ultimately steers us towards the idea that redemption is a choice, but one that requires true self-awareness and the willingness to change.

Essay 2: How does Dickens use the Cratchit family to explore social injustice?

Thesis Statement
In *A Christmas Carol*, Dickens takes us on a journey of understanding, demonstrating how the Cratchit family represents the struggles of the poor in Victorian society. The Cratchits embody warmth, resilience, and family unity despite

their poverty, acting as a stark contrast to Scrooge's isolation and greed. The conflict between wealth and morality is evident in their interactions with Scrooge, as they show gratitude and generosity despite having very little, while he hoards his riches in bitterness. By the end of the novella, Dickens has steered us towards the idea that true wealth is found in human connection, not material possessions. One of the most powerful methods Dickens uses to present this theme is **contrast**, particularly in how he juxtaposes the Cratchits' joy with their suffering to highlight the cruelty of social inequality.

PASS Paragraph
Dickens presents the Cratchit family as a symbol of both poverty and resilience, using **contrast** to highlight their struggles against the indifference of the wealthy. When Dickens describes their Christmas dinner, he writes: *"There never was such a goose... Bob said he didn't believe there ever was such a goose cooked. Its tenderness and flavour, size and cheapness, were the themes of universal admiration."* The juxtaposition between **cheapness** and **admiration** shows how the Cratchits find joy in the smallest things, reinforcing the idea that wealth does not equate to happiness. However, Dickens also emphasises their suffering, particularly through Tiny Tim, whose frail condition is described through the **tragic foreshadowing** of *"If these shadows remain unaltered by the Future, the child will die."* This moment highlights the harsh realities of poverty, suggesting that the inaction of the rich directly contributes to the suffering of the poor. A Victorian audience, living in a time of great economic disparity, would have recognised Dickens' critique of a society that prioritises profit over people. Through this contrast, Dickens ultimately steers us towards the idea that social injustice is not inevitable, but a result of human choices—and, like Scrooge, society must change.

Essay 3: How does Dickens use the Ghost of Christmas Yet to Come to build tension and fear?

Thesis Statement

In *A Christmas Carol,* Dickens takes us on a journey of understanding, showing how fear can be a powerful force for change. The Ghost of Christmas Yet to Come is the most terrifying of the spirits, using silence and ominous imagery to confront Scrooge with the consequences of his actions. The conflict between ignorance and awareness is central to this moment, as Scrooge begins to realise that his choices have shaped his future, yet he still clings to a hope of redemption. By the end of this encounter, Dickens has steered us towards the idea that fear can act as a catalyst for transformation, forcing individuals to confront their deepest regrets. One of the most powerful methods Dickens uses in this stave is **personification**, as he transforms death and fate into tangible forces that physically haunt Scrooge.

PASS Paragraph

Dickens presents the Ghost of Christmas Yet to Come as a **terrifying embodiment of fate**, using **personification** to emphasise the inevitability of death and moral reckoning. The spirit is described as *"shrouded in a deep black garment, which concealed its head, its face, its form, and left nothing of it visible save one outstretched hand."* The imagery of **shrouding** aligns the ghost with **death itself**, as shrouds are traditionally used to cover the dead. The **outstretched hand**, silent yet commanding, reinforces the idea that fate is inescapable, urging Scrooge towards his final lesson. Later, when Scrooge sees his neglected grave, Dickens uses a **chilling rhetorical question** to heighten his desperation: *"Am I that man who lay upon the bed?"* This moment forces both Scrooge and the reader to confront mortality and the question of how one's life will be remembered. A Victorian audience, many of whom were deeply religious, would have viewed this scene as a stark warning about the consequences of greed and moral corruption. Dickens ultimately steers us towards the idea that fear can be transformative—it strips away illusion and forces people to acknowledge uncomfortable truths, paving the way for redemption.

Example Of An Essay With The Pass Method Incorporated Into The Analysis:

In A Christmas Carol, we go on a journey of understanding how family represents love, warmth, and human connection—something Scrooge has denied himself. By the end of the novella, Dickens may have wanted us to consider that family is not just a source of comfort, but also a moral guide, showing Scrooge what he has lost through his own choices.

The **conflict** in the novel lies between Scrooge's self-imposed isolation and the joy of familial bonds, with the Cratchits embodying the love he has rejected. The **mood shifts** from denial and refusal to realisation and regret, ultimately leading to Scrooge's redemption.

The **universal concepts** of love, isolation, and redemption drive this transformation. When viewed through the **lens** of Victorian social values, we find ourselves asking: Does true happiness come from wealth, or from the relationships we nurture?

One of the **most powerful methods** Dickens uses to present the importance of family is contrast, particularly between Scrooge and the Cratchits. In this extract, the Cratchits' home is depicted as full of warmth and unity, despite their poverty, highlighting the richness of their love in contrast to Scrooge's cold, isolated existence.

The **semantically linked** words "warm", "bless", and "cheer" evoke a sense of emotional abundance, **reinforcing for the reader** the idea that true wealth lies in human connection. In contrast, Scrooge's life is marked by words such as "solitary", "cold", and "neglected", symbolising his emotional deprivation and **steering the reader** towards an understanding of his isolation.

Literally, this contrast demonstrates how family provides love and support, even in hardship. **Metaphorically**, the Cratchits' modest meal represents contentment and gratitude, challenging the Victorian obsession with material wealth. The noun "warmth" not only refers to the physical heat of their home but also **symbolises** the emotional warmth they share, something Scrooge lacks. **Emotionally**, the reader is encouraged to sympathise with the Cratchits and feel pity for Scrooge, whose choices have left him devoid of such happiness.

Through this contrast, **Dickens reveals the moral lesson** that wealth is meaningless without love. He emphasises that Scrooge's journey towards redemption begins when he acknowledges this. The Cratchits portray the ideal family, showing generosity and kindness even in poverty, whereas Scrooge exaggerates the consequences of greed, serving as a warning.

Dickens ultimately steers us towards the realisation that family is the foundation of true happiness, posing the question: Is it ever too late to change and embrace love?

Printed in Dunstable, United Kingdom